GRAINS OF SAND

Poems of love, longing, and landscapes

COLTON BABLADELIS

This publication is a creative work protected in full by all applicable copyright laws, as well as by misappropriation, trade secret, unfair competition, and other applicable laws. No part of this book may be reproduced or transmitted in any manner without written permission from Winter Goose Publishing, except in the case of brief quotations embodied in critical articles or reviews. All rights reserved.

Winter Goose Publishing
45 Lafayette Road #114
North Hampton, NH 03862

www.wintergoosepublishing.com
Contact Information: info@wintergoosepublishing.com

Grains of Sand

COPYRIGHT © 2016 by Colton Babladelis

First Edition, November 2016

Cover Design by Winter Goose Publishing
Typesetting by Odyssey Books

ISBN: 978-1-941058-57-2

Published in the United States of America

For my father, for everything

Contents

In a Grain of Sand	1
I Lost My Words	4
To Listen	5
Droplets of Sun	6
Between the Day and Night	7
To Paint a Song	8
Reflections of Yourself	9
Of Waves in Paros	11
Asking About Absence	12
Of Love and War	15
In Ink and Blood (Salonika Rebetiko)	16
Abandoned	18
Quiriguá	19
The Magic of an Isle	20
A Smile in the Wind	22
Seeds of Love	24
From My Hands	25
A Fragile Package	26
A Reflection of Yours	27
Under a Brilliant Sun	29
But to Listen	30
Grain by Grain	31
Through Old Eyes	32
The Worth of a Word	34

The Words Came	35
Of Future Memories	37
La Media Naranja	38
Looking at Each Other	39
On the Lips of the Wind	40
Summer's Garden	41
Lovely Advice	42
Two Hearts	43
To Capture Time	44
Centuries Spent	45
To Love the Sky	47
To Dream of Your Memory	48
Untiring, Unceasing	50
Dark Skies	51
Time Through the Eyes of the Gods	52
Voices Resonate	54
The Hunger of the Dawn	55
The Nature of Coming and Going	56
Within the Nautilus	57
An Empty Bed	58
The Fury of the Gods	59
In Absence	60
In Essence of Memory	61
Upon an Old Shelf	62
Reincarnation	63
An Alley by Night	64

Words Escaped	65
To Say Goodbye	66
Rioja	67
Haunted Paths	68
When Fate Decides	69
To Survive on Hope	70
Broken Promises	71
Song of Stars	72
Time Falls	73
Now, Here	74
Slumbering Volcano	75
Monoliths	76
Emerald Blanket	77
The Desert's Secrets	78
Steam Over Picaya	79
Macedonian Conquest	80
The Voice of the Sea	81
Found There, in the Islands	82
Salonica by Night	83
An Old Traveler	84
ACKNOWLEDGMENTS	85
ABOUT THE AUTHOR	86

In a Grain of Sand

"Let's walk," you told me.
So we went through the old and rocky avenues.
We spoke about the life
of a grain of sand
and all of its journeys,
and all of the places it knows.
"The memories in those eyes,
are broader than time itself."

And when I touched it,
I felt a past
that started in the stars
and flew through time
in its fixed and celestial path.
I absorbed the most partial fragment
of the capacity of its vision and sixth sense
weaving an infinite fabric.

I heard the ephemeral voice of eternity,
and I saw the youthful face of Father Time.
I shook the hand
of kings and peasants alike.
Centuries of pain,
millennia of joy
are a compound current, firm and sure,
a wire through every organism,
that breathes, has breathed, and continues to breathe,
the electricity flowing
through a web alive with conscious instincts.

I realized
that everything alive reflects the energy
of everything else,
and contains innumerable pieces
of the mosaic of souls
that walk through life
with the same hopes
and the same beginnings.

I read a chapter of the universal book
written by this grain of sand,
and it told me of history
that encompasses everything in the view of the stars.

And I saw the peak of every mountain
and the bottom of every river.
I felt the breath upon my neck
expelled by every lover
in a rush of forbidden love.
I felt the sting of grief
leaving so many pains
even if the most transient.

I saw the sun rise in the arms of the early morning,
and I watched the eternal sunset as it darkened above the round earth.
I was the leaf of the venerable oak
that falls with the colors every autumn,
the fresh lives of the first day of spring,
a snowflake, unique in my frozen design,
the happiness and freedom of a wave in the sea under the summer sun.

I was the celestial calendar
that only abides by the dark and unbreakable laws,
and the second that persists
in the first kiss of soulmates.
I was the roots and the branches
of the tree of life,
and the spark that starts the fire of love
that will burn the walls of time,
and the limits of the sky.

In a grain of sand,
I took into myself everything that is
and everything else took me in,
together we exist,
and we continue linked.

I Lost My Words

On a windswept castle
Perched above a glittering village
A volcanic wind blew through our hair
And smelled of forgotten words

In a loud bar
Full of suits and ties
10,000 miles across the world
We spun on a humid dance floor

Atop an old castle
I lost my words
As I held you against my chest

On a scorched red beach
I found letters among the sand
Syllables washed ashore among the waves

Under an unrelenting sun
I found more than I had known possible
And I learned to say everything without a word

To Listen

I only want to listen
while you aren't speaking
because in the silence
you tell me more than all of the intricate words
that you sing to me
and I hear the depth of your heart
and I see everything that you love
and I understand everything that you desire
and everything that you wish for.
Because in a moment
the silence tells us more
than a thousand stories
filled with nonsense.

Droplets of Sun

I saw a beam of sun
wink at me
before it crashed
full force
into a petal
full of deep blue veins
and with this solar warmth
exuded a fragrance so sweet
that we became intoxicated
and threw around heavy words
and forgot to keep our vigilance,
and so we fell
with the sunshine
and became drunk with love and passion
deep into the black night,
and awoke as droplets of dew
to the hopes on a new horizon.

Between the Day and Night

Like day and night
we were bound back to back,
lashed by the laws of love,
understood only by the moon
and the sun.
We existed forever
me illuminating your hauntingly deep eyes
and you eclipsing me
in your moments of splendor.
We shared a belief
that there was nothing more sacred
than the earth below us
and without her wonders,
our circulation would be in vain.
Born of ancient stars
that once flitted and frolicked,
formed from a battle older than time,
halves split forever to roam the skies,
from the moment we needed each other
we were cursed
to only ever catch cosmic glances.
Twins we were called,
although lovers we really were
from eons of longing.

To Paint a Song

You asked me about love,
and I told you about life,
I explained the emotion
but how is it possible to convey the moment?
You gave me your hands
so that I could show you what it feels like,
but I took your ear
and tried to mimic the whispers
sweet like sun drops that you gave to me.
You told me to paint it,
so that you could understand through a picture,
but from my fingertips came a song
full of color and rhymes
that carried a tune light with joy
that lasted but a moment.
You asked why it was so fleeting,
and I told you it went nowhere,
for the forest sang the lyrics
and the sea provided the music,
and at that instant you understood,
that love travels like a wave,
and grows like a sequoia.

Reflections of Yourself

Do you see yourself in me
when we walk amongst the leaves,
while we gaze to the stars
that blanket our home in soft light?

Do you see yourself in me
as I grow into a man,
as I learn to bear
the weight of the world,
as you have done,
like Atlas before you?

Do you see yourself in me
as we both gasp in the crisp morning air,
as we bask in a waning light,
as we loosen our grip
on the day?

I see myself in you
when I greet the dewy morning,
while I breathe white star light
from the words around me
as I wait for the world to turn.

I see myself in you
as I teach others
to plant the seeds of love
to water them with humor.

I see myself in you
as I greet the night
like an old and loyal friend
the color of a wistful youth.

Of Waves in Paros

You asked me if you are a wave.
I quickly replied yes,
but implored you to stay
even though it doesn't come naturally.

You remained still,
whether of interest or apathy.

Because, yes,
you are a wave to me
with the rhythm of a sunbeam
and the passion
of a hurricane.

And the rogue wave that you are,
in a single instant,
capsized my boat
and left me floating,
stranded and confused
with nothing but the words in my throat.

As I dive deep to the floor
your pressure eases me down
and asserts that you're more,
not just a wave,
but the whole of the sea.

Asking About Absence

"What is absence?" she asked him.
She knew not the word,
but the feeling was familiar.

It crept over her,
a fog thicker than her accent
it blinded everything but her fear.

The word first came to her on the lips of the moon,
bemoaning her loneliness in the absence of the sun,
filling the empty fog with a silvery hue.

"Have no worries," he repeated to her.
"The time will pass,
faster than the stars above."

She watched the stars dance across the sky,
their light and the heat of the sand
was all that kept her company.

The night told the day of her void
and so the sun filled her days with brilliant heat
and though it warmed her, it did not fill the space.

She asked the air for advice,
and the wind blew her ghosts of jasmine
his words came with each floating petal.

She knew the absence well,
a hundred humid nights made them intimate,
a hundred breathless days made them enemies.

It accompanied her to the shore
where the sea whispered to her every day
and the foam of the waves left stories in the sand.

It eventually consumed her dreams,
making the twilight as lonely as the dawn
and blinding her memory with deceitful apparitions.

"And what is time?" he asked her rhetorically,
for he knew the answer
whether it be true or solely reassurance.

He spoke in circles
around days and nights
around the difficulties it brought.

His words tamed her loneliness,
for the sea could whisper to her
but the waves carried his love.

"I'll send you my senses," he offered up.
"My words will echo from the clouds
with shining sights and sounds."

His letters sang to her,
envelopes arrived, sealed with hope,
and carried on wings of desire.

The lyricism of the words shadowed the absence,
his songs rose over the depths of the night
and broke the day with the sun.

His words were strong and clear,
he threw them into the wind
and waited for them to reach her.

He aspired to reach her through his dreams,
a hundred nights of profound meditation,
a hundred days of frenzied inspiration.

Equally as scared
he let neither the absence
nor the loneliness take root.
He looked to the sky as she looked to the water
until the absence was met by laughter
that colored the sunset orange.

Of Love and War

Days of love
and nights of war
as the sun hugs you
and gives you confidence
the moon gazes at you
with eyes full of doubts.
The distance is our battle
a summer passes by us, passes in the distance.

Days of love
and nights of war
as the humid jungle tells me
stories of ages lost
and the desert gives you
stories of love caked in sand.
I send you letters made of my words
to ease the pain of the distance.

Hope and warmth
are the enemies of the fear
that comes to you in the night.
Over ten thousand miles
my thoughts flew to you
above waves in an ocean
that occupies the spaces of your heart.
You cried to me when the rains came
that you could no longer control the storm.
Forty days of love float on the horizon,
forty nights of war threaten us from behind.

In Ink and Blood (Salonika Rebetiko)

I leave you my words
That you love me more
My body will age
My face will fall
My tongue will fail
But my words will remain
In ink and blood
And I will love nothing more
Than your words and your ideas
The roads you've walked
The places you've seen
Your touch and your body
Only alive but for a moment
Your eyes will cloud
With memories of days gone by
And your lips will slow
With the weariness of the years
Our bones will turn to dust
As we wear through the soles of our shoes
The sun will burn holes in our skin
And the moon will drive us crazy
With nights of passion
That last an eternal moment
And in those moments
Those splendorous days
And those wondrous nights
Dizzy, and tied within ourselves
Remember the words

Give me your soul
Spill your essence
In ink and blood
For only your words will I love
Tell me what you seek
In the sky and sea we will search for answers
Find them we will not
But words, those will come
In abundance they will fall
And as they fall, so will we
Deep, into a state of darkness
Deep, as a light shines upon us
And words we will have
Words I will give you
In ink and blood
Words only will I take from you
In ink and blood
Manifest will be the time
On paper our words will fall
In time our bodies will rot
In time our faces will be forgotten
In time our words will live
In time our love will be known
In ink and blood

Abandoned

From Filoktitis' cave
To a stranded ship
An island left
Somewhere between the shores of Troy
And the pain of Anatolia
Fettered to a distant Greece
Through language and myth
Forsaken in the sea
Beaten by the wind
We landed on her shores
Two hearts forgotten by our bodies
Two hearts that could not forget each other
On different ships we arrived
Solitary and weary
Covered in years of salty tears
The fates sent clouds above us
Billows of sweet water came down
Washing our darkened skin
And quenched the thirst of desire
Abandoned by the gods
Forgotten by men and time alike
All but the wind and the sea had gone
And in the absence
Where all had been abandoned
We filled our hands with her soil
And our hearts with a divine song

Quiriguá

In the place of the dragonflies
I spoke with gods dethroned
But not entirely forgotten
I picked avocados and mangos
Ripe and dripping
With stories waiting to be told
I walked in ancient footsteps
Of scholars, kings, and warriors
Whose voices echo from the jungle ruins
I drifted into a light sleep
Filled with visions disconnected from time
Fueled by the humid jungle air

The Magic of an Isle

for James Wells

Oh! The magic of an isle,
from Greece to Ireland
to the straits of Mackinac,
the wonder they instill,
a love back in port,
a new horizon over the bow,
a new land, a fresh thrill,
time left behind,
folk of a different sort.

Oh! The magic of an isle,
where we all hope to find
a life anew,
a slower state of mind,
a language only the heart can speak,
a place only the soul can fly,
lay my body on her shores
in morning mists
and afternoon sunshine.

Oh! The magic of an isle,
in her mountains we found solace,
in her streets we found the past,
alleyways long grown over,
fertile fields and sacred hills,
glasses brimmed with friendship,

a peace unmatched by all mankind,
dreams of rolling hills
and the voices of spirits in every stone.

Oh! The magic of an isle,
from Greece to Ireland,
one day our boat will dock,
one day we'll turn that soil,
one day we'll breathe that air,
one day we'll have our own,
one day we'll meet with god,
one day we'll see our isle,
that day will be sublime.

A Smile in the Wind

The power of a smile
has nothing equal
such as the potential
in the language of laughter.

What is stronger
than a shared connection
between two strangers
over a light joke?

Those that live
with a smile across their faces,
I am sure,
travel through life with the most luck.

The sound of peace
is carried on the wings
of a laugh
that escaped the lips of lovers.

If you listen,
as I have surely done,
you can hear the sky
laughing in the wind.

Because the face of the world smiles
when the sun shines upon all
and dreams fly limitless
under a full moon.

So, if you ask the mountains,
they will answer you with confidence
that the rivers and the lakes
flood the earth with sweet sentiments.

But only those that listen
to the secrets of the wind
know where internal peace
actually resides.

Seeds of Love

The enlightened
they wanted to be,
they spoke of revelations
of turns of love
of changes to be made.
They made plans
and planned to make changes,
the world would be different
they said.
They would spread the seeds,
step by step,
over the cold and cracked earth,
over the desert sands
and throughout the anonymous cities,
they would lead by example,
and show the world how to love.

From My Hands

From my hands I forged you a heart
Carved from Parian marble
And wrought from the fire and iron of
Hephaestus

From my hands I brought you flowers
Sown from seeds of love and triumph
And fed with water glittering with hope

From my hands I sent you my words
Inscribed into the wind itself
And given wings by the pang of longing

In my hands I took your heart
Full to the seams of youthful pride
And bursting with anticipation for the impending fall

A Fragile Package

I am made huge
With the universe inside me
Your arms hardly reach around my waist
Yet they encircle my love
My heart held silently
As if tied tightly within a package
And held between your gentle hands
Waiting to undo the knots
That diligently guarded
A feeble thud-thud
Time pranced upon your lips
As you slowly opened the box
That had long held me silent
Then, I could see the sun
And I swelled towards the horizon

A Reflection of Yours

We couldn't wait any longer,
this the gods knew.
So they gave us two mirrors,
little reflective gifts in themselves
that truly possessed nothing of a proper reflection,
but rather brought us together.
We saw each other in the ceilings of our bedrooms
and told of exotic journeys,
of weekends spent on beaches or in deserts,
of expeditions through magical forests
and of ancient spirits
that we have met.
This secret, mine,
this mirror,
in its reflection
where my face should be
I see nothing but your smile.
For this I have changed myself,
and have learned to take advantage of those surreal dreams
that the reflection of you
gives me every evening.
In an unsure state
I continue on,
in a realm seeming,
of travels without gravity,
but that were still in a certain orbit,
and everything that I see
every night in the limitless reflection

through which you gaze at me,
is you,
the girl in my pupil.

Under a Brilliant Sun

Kissed by the sun
you danced across the landscape
and I watched in amazement
as every part,
> your feet,
> your hair,
> your eyes,
> your dreams,
fluttered and flourished
and when we touched,
we melted,
for the brilliant sun
had softened both of us,
and we could no longer tell
if the salt on our lips was from the sea,
or from making love under the sun.

But to Listen

I only want to listen,
so speak to me for a moment,
tell me all the stories
that you've polished and glistened.
Your words are what entice me,
painting your world in my eyes,
and from the tip of my pen
your history comes alive.
For your words are what I will fall in love with
so speak to me of clear skied nights,
where our dreams outnumbered the stars
or lazy summer days
with humid winds saturated in lust.

Grain by Grain

He looked to the sand,
and grain by grain
he gathered eons and epochs
of days gone by,
entire histories covered and forgotten,
and heard the voices of love
and of lives
spent in the scorching sun.

Through Old Eyes

His old eyes did see
a little too much.
They had done a once over
of just about everything under the sun.
Years ago they gave out,
and simply stopped seeing the good.
His eyes became hard,
his tone bitter at times,
and he proudly claimed
that his tongue had spent all its pleasantries.
His hands had toiled at one too many jobs,
years of labor worn into his bones,
a body made large and able
and a quick temper even bigger
made tough in bars and marinas.
His good humor had never left, though,
leaving a brilliant mind shining,
fell victim to time
and the condition of illness
that seems to plague mere mortals.
A condition that shocked him more than the sickness itself.
His old eyes did see
everything there was to do
and everything there was left,
and at that moment
they became fatigued
and everything else followed
from the eyes to the knees

to his back
to his hands and feet
until all the pain
a life worked to the bone
stopped in his mind
and manifested on his face.
The universe knows well your soul
and reciprocates your charge,
and like a touch it will push,
and he knew well his limits,
met somewhere along the roads
that walk time and pain
hand in hand.

The Worth of a Word

She asked,
"What is the worth of a promise?"
with a heart full of hope
but eyes that had seen too much
and ears that had heard too many deceptions.
"A word is but a word,"
the reply came from within,
"And in it there can be no value,"
for he too knew the tyranny of lies,
the madness induced by an empty promise.
Unless a person has nothing
but his word and his action,
for that I have,
and have found what I lacked,
in honesty is fulfillment,
and in time there is trust.
I cannot force away your fears,
but I can endure a lifetime
to prove the worth of my word.

The Words Came

My words filled the air
And took root in your ears
And took form in front of your eyes

They filled your lungs
And fueled your desire
And enveloped your body in sweet security

They came from the sea
One at a time, each with a wave
Crashing over you, and lapping on the shore of your skin

They came with the wind
Blown down the mountains
Whispering secrets learned from the sky

Words spoken in tongues long forgotten
And written in scripts never deciphered
All carrying the same sweet aroma

Words came in the rains
They poured down in daily waves
And flooded every corner of your mind

Words that shone with the sun
And fed flowers and man alike
Warm with love and hope

They bounced from the walls
Built so high by men
And tumbled buildings quicker than bombs

They performed miracles
As they invoked the gods
And soothed the ears of dying souls

They freed the masses
And young minds alike
As they formed and reshaped the future

Words heavy on the lips of lovers
Words that created worlds
Words that evaded time

Of Future Memories

I sit in reverence to your past
Thankful for everything that came before me
What you have seen I do not know
What you have felt, I cannot fathom
What you have become, I have come to love
A collection of moments
Fragmentary and beautiful
Strung together by joy and pain
From your past materializes your present
I found you in the reflection of yesterday
With your face looking forward
In this moment we exist
We gave tomorrow to Eros
And forsake yesterday in regret
Our tongues lapped the dew of today
The sticky sweet taste of hope
In a morning bursting with flavor
We drank the bitter nostalgia
Of lessons hard learned
And groped in the darkness
For a day yet to come
I fell into a deep pool of your past
And learned to love an untold future
As we lived for every moment
We breathed in the reality of us

La Media Naranja

In but a moment
We gained a lifetime
Every step uncovered new sights
Every night new heights
At first glance we fell
At first touch we rose
Lifted by a joy
Accumulated through an eon together
A story of reincarnation
Known by many names
Told by many tongues
Dreamt through many nights
We again came together
Two halves of the same orange

Looking at Each Other

Our eyes loved each other
As one peered into the other
A golden brown reflection
Of a mysterious chestnut
A mirror looking back at itself
Wondering when it started to look so beautiful
And where its edges broke
And where infinity started

On the Lips of the Wind

You wanted to speak of eternity
But I could only think of this moment
Because to you, love is a stone
Forming an ever present monolith
A peak on the horizon
Your star that would always lead me home
An anchor to hold you to the earth
But to me love was ephemeral like the wind
It changes with the seasons
A powerful and awe inspiring storm
My dusty and worn pathway around the world
It is what lifts me off my feet
And for a moment I climbed on your mountain
And you were battered by the storm I carried
But in time the storm passed
And the walls of your mountain crumbled
My pathway led back home
As I followed your loving stars
The wind blows from all directions
Always on its lips
My love for you

Summer's Garden

Two lovers met in a garden
Late in a humid summer
The air dripped with lust
Full of a sweet aroma
Where roses bloomed eternally
And ripe figs fell to their feet
In a garden, love was planted
And in this garden, love grew

Lovely Advice

Like the night
comes to the day,
fall in love,
slowly, all at once.
As the sun sets on the horizon
dream quickly
of past peace
but keep your eyes
open to future delights

Two Hearts

Where does one begin
and the other end?
A seamless road
between two worlds,
a disparate night,
a fruitful day,
in the margins
I wonder—
Whose heart is whose?

To Capture Time

He could think of nothing less
than to give her the world,
so out of words he built the cosmos.
He created new senses.
He captured time itself,
and set to filling her world
with the essence of happiness.
Above all, he needed time first,
what is a world,
or a life shared
that lacks time eternal?
He looked to the sand,
and grain by grain
he gathered eons and epochs
of days gone by,
entire histories covered and forgotten,
and heard the voices of love
and of lives
spent in the scorching sun.

Centuries Spent

I could easily explore until eternity
the curves of your body.
A year per finger,
a year per toe.
I would spend a decade
with my head upon your lap
and another on the small of your back.
It would take a century
to make my way up your legs
and to your breasts,
caressing every curve
for a few years
just to prove that every part
is equally as smooth.
A millennium would pass
as I traced the bow of your lips,
trying in vain to sketch
every expression that passed
over your tongue and teeth
and left with an effort through your lips.
Your eyes,
and your hair,
are where
time would fall away from me
and in the reflections
of your black eyes
would stare back colors
made by prisms long hidden from the eyes of men,

and I would begin to count
every strand of hair,
for though black and uniform they seem,
each one is colored by the stories of your youth,
and eons spent under the sun,
lazily discussing matters of love and art.
Each story would play out
and from those a million more
until one, two, three eternities
had passed and I would be ancient,
but wise by the knowledge
bestowed by your body,
and my eyes had lived to see
works of art in your honor.

To Love the Sky

Although the sun came
From a world of light and warmth
And the moon knew nothing more
Than the frigid solitude of midnight
They both loved the same sky
As if the winds
Were the solitary voice of longing
And the clouds drifted by
Like the lofty dreams so lucid
For from that expansive heaven
They both returned to the same horizon
They kissed the same earth
One leaving it parched and wanting
The other drenched and tired
Those two were born
Loving the same sky

To Dream of Your Memory

I slipped into a dream
and fell into your presence,
an ephemeral memory,
an eternal desire,
quietly, silently, without words
you spoke to me, asked me of love,
asked me of time, of the persistence of memory.
The sun broke the delirium,
the city came awake around me.
Slowly, you faded
as I fought to maintain your memory,
my senses struggled to keep a piece,
first failed my sight,
and I lost your face
as my eyes opened to a whitewash ceiling,
as the tingling of morning subsided
I lost the feel of you next to me
and the delicate drag
of your nails across my back,
the soft murmur of your voice
tried to keep me in a dream
and the aroma of your skin
kept me dazed until the sunset,
every blink was a kiss,
every time I opened my eyes
a dagger entered my heart,
every night you came to me
and every morning I could taste your lips.

A memory from afar.
A dream from within.
A pain from the deep.
A love that crossed an ocean.

Untiring, Unceasing

Waves fell onto the beach
Resting their weary heads
Asking the sand for forever
And the meaning of the day
As the sand conjured a history
Buried deep in time and stone
Of a love that moved the very land
That made the ground reach to the sky
And the gods cry
As lightening and thunder crashed
And the waves realized
That the sand was always there
Unceasing and untiring
The ocean has always laid its head
On the lap of its shores
And so will I forever be everywhere
For you to lay your head upon my lap

Dark Skies

Rolling, rolling
It crashed over the horizon

They listened
But their fear couldn't silence the thunder

It rained
And they saw the world in every drop

A reflection
That stared back with cold eyes

The storm
Blew away all the tired monotony

In it
The whirlwind and excitement she sought

They laughed
Because they saw the beauty in the destruction

They left
Because they knew they had found what they came for

And wandered
Searching for another answer
To a question
That neither had ever asked

Time Through the Eyes of the Gods

And in a moment
we realized that time didn't exist
for we had lived something eternal
in this life so ephemeral.

We asked the sky
who lightly laughed back
and winked at us with warm eyes,
and whispered over the sea and through the leaves,

"That time was nothing more
than a construction, an imposition
of lonely and broken-hearted men
so that they could count the tangible seconds
of lamentation.

But it was never intended for us,
so light of heart
and pure of soul
who knew not the feeling
of familiarity that the constraints of time,
the enemy of eternity,
had shackled upon the minds,
hearts,
souls,
and bodies
of the mortals.

For as you two know not
the plight of the plebeians,
they know not
the freedom that you have been bestowed,
nor the joy that you exude
nor the defiance of time itself
that has been emboldened in you
by the profundity of your belief,
by the strength of the chords of your love."

Voices Resonate

As each drop slams into the tin roof above,
each one a piece,
each another bit of the puzzle,
I meet each one,
and they all tell me
of the fear they had before they fell.
They told me they didn't understand
why we liked such a dry world.
They told me of their life in the clouds
drifting above the sea
and the mountain
winking at open volcanoes
high above earthly preoccupations.
They told me that they only fall
when a soul finds pieces of itself,
for we're all just pieces from the beginning,
vessels waiting to be filled.
They told me how we're all just waiting,
waiting to be filled.

The Hunger of the Dawn

My eyes saw the breaking dawn
Smiling over the face of the horizon
A curve upon your hip
Glimpses in the early morning
A smile lay upon your lips
A gentle present
Remaining from times gone by
Sustaining only in your deepest dreams
He knew what her eyes wanted to say
Before her mouth knew the words
They spoke a special language
Borne from the heart
A waking kiss on the shoulder
Sets the air into vibration
That cannot be calmed
Until they lay again tonight
A trail left upon your skin
Under the gentle pressure of my finger
Stirs something deeper down
Than the hunger in her heart

The Nature of Coming and Going

Since I came,
I've been conquered
by grandiose dreams
that wandered into my soul
and by the temptation of lust
that you flaunted too freely.

Since you came,
you've been overcome
by emotions you couldn't control
and by sentiments in the air
finer than dust
that I tried to steal so greedily.

Since we left,
the rains have come and gone
and behind them is a trail of flowers
under which the pathways we frequented
thousands of petals
crafted by many hands in the wind
and painted by your desires.

Within the Nautilus

An endless circle
A spiral wound upon itself
A seamless world
Created within ourselves
Once we entered the labyrinth
Neither left the same
Although our bodies left the maze
Our hearts remained within
Our souls devoured by the depth
Our lives intertwined by the hope
Our bodies joined together
Our eyes looked into each other
Knowing what our mouths had asked
Our words fell like raindrops
Our hope rose with the sun

An Empty Bed

I left an empty bed
In a house filled with pain
A desk covered in dust
Neglected for years too long
We mended all the wounds
And planted seeds of hope
In a garden strewn with friendship
As I took a bitter goodbye
After but a moment in your glory
Fate smiled upon my soul
And threw her chains about our hearts
An ocean was but a drop
Drying under a noon day sun
A light that darkened our skin
And baked us into the same mold
Every step drew us closer
Every dream brought your scent
As you lay your head upon my pillow
We filled an empty bed

The Fury of the Gods

Fixed on the horizon
Our eyes locked onto the light
Days on a rough sea
Played tricks on our minds
As our legs began to cope
We waited for a calm that never came
As frothy waves washed our hope away
A half moon half laughed
As the seabirds cried in vain
The salty air left our lips parched
And our souls hungry
We welcomed in the storm
As we scorned away the sky
And Zeus cast his thunderbolts
As Poseidon unleashed his fury
Upon a bed of rocks we crashed
Bloodied by the voyage
We drank in the celestial night
As we cast away the abysmal darkness

In Absence

We learned not to blink
That sleep merely transported us
From day to day, from night to night
And that after long enough
Day and night were but words
That named the moods
That named the waves of joy
And the depths of fear
We no longer saw time
Moments became forgotten to our memory
We no longer heard anything
But the lapping of the days
Against the walls of our hearts
And from season to season
We gained a fresh start
Behind us we left histories
Laden in sorrow and regret
Our sails caught winds
Of fresh desires and dreams
That pushed us towards new destinies
Of castles perched over the sea
And sunsets that painted every soul orange

In Essence of Memory

The weight of your memory
Held by my struggling eyes
Renewed daily by the things you left behind
We live in but a moment
We love for a brief eternity
Our words live
And our words die
In a single murmur
Our story survives the tests of time
What is our memory
But an imprint of our souls
Left to walk the earth
In the hearts of those
Too tortured to forget
A word passed from mouth to mouth
A solitary story heard by every ear thereafter

Upon an Old Shelf

The things you left me
Are scattered about the floor
Fallen from their places
Forgotten after years upon a shelf
Everything you've given me
Shattered in a day
I broke it all without a thought
So that I could build you something more
From the pieces of your time
And the shards of your love
I built us a new body
Constructed of sweat and soul

Reincarnation

I've lived a thousand years
Filled with a thousand loves
All in the shape of your face
Graced by the same smile
Uncountable nights in your embrace
Wrapped in a blanket of your hair
Millennia learning the arts
Sketches in stone
Poems that fell timelessly
Tongues dead in time
That whispered words
Forgotten to the ages
All telling the same story
All carrying the same tone
Bodies pushed to wander
Forced to swim in the currents of memory
To walk the deserted lands of sorrow
Until one soul finds the other

An Alley by Night

A blurred light,
a hurried kiss.
That wind, oh that wind!
The lonely sting of night
cut by jasmine
and mingled with the perfume on your neck.
As stones fell around us
the smoke cleared from our eyes,
our hearts, and our lips,
and that wind played tricks.
As it lulled us to sleep
it carried our dreams to the clouds
and our souls to each other.

Words Escaped

Like a message in a bottle
It wasn't ever meant to be read
A word thrown to the wind
It meant what it was supposed to
And before it could take hold
Before those roots that dove so deep
As if to consume the entirety of the vessel
Stretched down to those sweet waters
A wave came on the shoulders
Of a wind bitter and acrid
A late December sun lifted its eyelids
And looked disapprovingly at the shore
And so once again, agonizingly
I tore those words out of the air
I burned the space they left
And filled it with dreams of you

To Say Goodbye

I was never able to say *goodbye*
My mouth refused to let the words escape
And my heart always held them too dear
For your perfume hung in my memories
And wafted sweet and slow
Into every corner of every day
Until I forgot how or why
I had first wanted to utter
Such melancholic and severing syllables
And I realized why
My mouth could not say the words
And why my heart swelled
When your name was mentioned
And my tears flowed
When I felt your pain

Rioja

Tinted
Everything was a shade of red
Droplets on my collar
As if my very life blood has spilled
Circles on all my notes
The bottom of an overused glass
Of fading ideas and painful memories
My own lenses
Drown in the glitter of the bottom of that glass
Everything smelled of crushed rose petals
And stale wine barrels
Dripping in youthful romance
And the night's infidelities with the day
Red was the morning on the first of spring
And red were my eyes in mourning
Red were the nights of early summer
As our skin became flushed with defiance and longing
And our lips became stained
With the deep purple hue of loss

Haunted Paths

Ghosts walked those paths
Leaving bitter wisps of dust behind
In that city they could not find rest
Nor could their hearts find solace
Their struggle rode the wings of twilight
Their cries haunted the night
Memories eternal
Memories of transgressions from a past life
Pained by the thought of lost perfection
They threw themselves into sorrow
As a lover casts himself into the ocean
For so long the darkness was their friend
That they came to fear happiness
As if joy was a precursor to betrayal
Those paths were haunted by their footsteps
Until their love let the pain finally rest

When Fate Decides

Two lost souls
Cast into the world
One cold, the other lonely
Serendipity smiled upon them
And for a brief moment
Their fates aligned
But the sun rose
And by compulsion they moved
Although a piece was always there
Always where it had been
That piece was called hope
And in time it grew
With suffering it flourished
With distance it grew patient
And when fate decided
Those souls found each other again

To Survive on Hope

Summer unfurled its sweet grasp
As the heat brought new blooms
My heart grew with the first petals of spring
Winter had been so harsh
It left us both marred and tired
It made us forget the smell of freedom
But something new faced the sun
Now, it knew where to look
For the sky I reached
For your memory I longed
In the moon I saw your face
I swear your voice sang in the evening breeze
Past the sunset you waited
In my garden, I stayed
My heart grew on hope alone

Broken Promises

Broken promises fell from their lips
And were swept away by the wind
Utterances of eternity
Lost in an abysmal night
In a moment the world was broken
As they dropped to their knees
Each star cried for them
A haunting melody of sorrow and joy
Of days spent in the shadow of love
And nights spent in the resplendence of loss
Days passed in a moment
Each night an eternity upon itself
Torn apart by nature
Brought together by fate

Song of Stars

The sun forgot to set
Because it missed the moon
Their love had come undone
But never was forgotten
For in her sullen face
The day so lit the night
And as the stars wept
Songs laden with summer dew
Melodies of memories
Taken away by the passing day
Carried from earth to sky
And from night to day
So too did the stars dance
For love became their only memory
And all they knew was joy

Time Falls

Time falls from the day
cascading from the past
like grains of sand from a hand,
hands filled with more than hope
desperately reaching for missed opportunities,
they found nothing to hold
but hands themselves.
Like the light holds the day's truths
and the dark holds the night's obscure desires,
so did time hold answers
that the sun inquired of the moon
and the sea of the waves,
inextricably linked
while eternally separated,
their hope knew no boundaries,
no border or limitations,
their hearts were made light
to float above the heaviness that absence imparted,
for although it could not be seen,
they were sure something more existed.

Now, Here

The ambience now,
here in Latin America,
holds in it something unique,
something refreshing and ancient,
the essence of its personality.
I found everything that I searched for,
in the land,
in the people,
in the songs,
in the night-covered streets.
The rains started,
and I
I needed those rains
to wash my hands
of years of difficulties,
of nights of terrors,
of travels filled with broken promises.
I invited the storm in,
because only under that loud tin roof
could I hear your laughter in my memory,
even though you are across an ocean,
in this now,
in this here,
you come to me in a dream
and seem to me something so much
as a shining apparition
of every star
that shines upon me every night.

Slumbering Volcano

The center, an open eye
A gaping crater
Staring back at me

Rimmed with embers
Throwing into the stillness
Hope and warmth

Like a distant voice

Calling out from a bygone day
And casting a shadow
On a sleepy and wine stained night

Where miniature globes
Of iridescence and immaturity
Danced around our bodies

Where laughter emanated
With a trembling roar
Awakening our souls

Monoliths

They stood alone
A testament to their knowledge
Faces turned to the sun
Pasts turned to the moon
They held hands for as long as possible
Until the years made their arms weary
Diluvial rains changed their form
And washed the dust from their bones
The solstice awoke their senses
And a singular flower bloomed from their hearts
A seed grew from hope
And the sweet aroma of love drifted into their minds

Emerald Blanket

Above a Northern Michigan sky
Softly sat the heavens
A twinkling infinity
So full of silence
That I could hear the voices
Of memories long forgotten
Ruminations on the world
An expansive emerald blanket
Enveloped me
Into its resin-soaked fibers
And upon a bed of needles
I became the night

The Desert's Secrets

Worn down after centuries of cohesion,
broken apart by nothing else than the elements.
What great travelers!
What timeless hermits!
To form the words of giants
and rob the works of masters,
infinite faces have heard
stories that changed the world
and seen tales die all in one breath,
for secrets told
and secrets kept
all fall eventually
into the baking sands.

Steam Over Picaya

Steam rises
From mountains that lament
Years of losses
And years of tears
For they've presided over people lost
And civilizations swallowed
By the jungle of conquest
And the monster of humanity

Macedonian Conquest

Across a sprawling plain
Rushed an army worn to the bone
Two vast spines, jagged and rocky
Divided by an alluvial vein
Sprang a desire to rule the world
From father to son
Borne from metal and fire
From those Northern Macedonian plains
Blew a wind of change
That smelled of blood and conquest
Triumph and sorrow
It carried the word of early death
Spoken in that old Greek tongue
A single name floated
From north to south, west to east
A sweet rejoice or a bitter resentment
The lips of the masses all rang out
For him, Alexander

The Voice of the Sea

A shell spoke to me
It told me of the sea
Of sirens and krakens
Of danger and depths
It told me of time
Lost to the sand
An eternal wave
Beating, beating
Against the shores of conscious
Of the lives lived and lost
To the fury of Poseidon
Of the men born to the sea
And those whose only love
Was her starry-eyed night

Found There, in the Islands

Was it just the island?
Was it solely the salty air,
the constant breeze,
the perfection of the sea,
the lack of time
that pressed us so fervently?

My temperament was changed,
amplified and augmented by the possibilities.
Oh how the muses sing to sailors only in passing!

As I am a catalyst,
so too shall this moment be,
for was it all but a spark
that began my realization
of what this land holds over me.

Salonica by Night

A city comes alive by night
A million lights
Lighting a million faces
A hundred languages flowing
From the lips of a port
Full of ancient commerce
Voices bouncing off other voices
All emanating from the White Tower
Memories of a vibrant past
Of calls to prayer
Of the ebb and flow
Of refugees and of a safe refuge
Over her ancient walls
Sprang a culture intertwined
Woven in dusty streets
And burned by the ravages of time

An Old Traveler

Oh, noble tortoise!
Venerated traveler!
The sand that you've seen
flow to the sea!
How do the waves sound
from beyond the horizon?
Where do you find peace
when your home is adrift?
From where did you come
and how long have you been gone?
Tell me of your home,
of swaying palms
and lonely beaches.

ACKNOWLEDGMENTS

I would like to thank my former professors for encouraging my writing, especially the Modern Greek department at the University of Michigan. I would also like to thank my mother for her continual support and for scrupulously reviewing my work.

ABOUT THE AUTHOR

Poet Colton Babladelis is a native of the Upper Peninsula of Michigan where he spent most of his childhood exploring the incredible forests, rivers, and lakes. His love of nature has found its way into most parts of his life, and surfaces in both his poetry and his work at the Erb Institute at the University of Michigan. Drawing inspiration from travel and diverse cultures and nature around the world, Colton strives to address the timeless dichotomies of the world: night and day, light and dark, love and hate.

www.ingramcontent.com/pod-product-compliance
Lightning Source LLC
Chambersburg PA
CBHW051348040426
42453CB00007B/468